A Dose Of Love

Simple words of wisdom for creating more love and less fear in your relationships.

Staci Welch-Bartley
&
Tom Bartley

Copyright © 2017
Lease On Love
All rights reserved.
ISBN: 1540854396
ISBN-13: 978-1540854391

DEDICATION

We dedicate this book to our beloved mothers: our first teachers of the importance of love and connection, who both eloquently spread a dose of love everywhere they traveled.

Elaine G. Welch-Singleton
June 18, 1932 - February 28, 2016

Suzanne Jane Brintzenhofe
September 11, 1929 - December 23, 2015

DEAR READER,

It is our hope these pages will inspire new thoughts and actions toward understanding and experiencing love and connection in your life, FIRST with yourself, and then with others. For it is the experience of connection that provides each of us the ability to grow and our souls to flourish.

We all have times in our lives when we need a dose of love for ourselves or someone who crosses our path may need a dose from us. We share these words with you in the hopes you will use them up, and then pass them along to others in need of a good, heaping dose of love.

Sending you extraordinary love and the power to create it today,

Tom & Staci Bartley

WE HAVE FANTASTIC NEWS!

You can receive daily inspiration and a new Dose of Love every Wednesday by following us on Instagram @leaseonlove

AND

Join us in our Daily Dose Of Love Community on Facebook to participate in our challenge experiences and to get some of the love, support, and friendship you're looking for right now!

You can join us here:
thedailydoseoflove.com

THANK YOU

Thank you to these beautiful souls who have supported and contributed their talents to not only this book, but to our entire Lease On Love body of work.

Brooke Brown: Graphic Design and Layout

Christina Pilz: Editing

Becky Boyd: Marketing

ABOUT THE AUTHORS

Tom and Staci Bartley are dedicated to inspiring and teaching individuals and couples to create new beginnings, build deeper connections, and experience extraordinary toe- tingling love in their lives.

Toe-tingling love is for everyone, not just for the lucky few, and is accomplished by developing and practicing new relationship skills.

Tom and Staci are also the creators of Lease On Love; an online platform offering courses, webinars, workshops, and books for all aspects of the relationship journey: single to married and back again.

To learn more about them, we invite you to visit their webpage at www.leaseonlove.com

#doseoflove

Ask yourself this question:
"Are you looking to be liked or are you looking for love?"

♡

Most of us are so disconnected we have forgotten how good it feels to live...or LOVE.

@leaseonlove

#doseoflove

In order to have personal boundaries, you need to claim a few!

> What if choices were not viewed as right and wrong, but instead as just a variety of life experiences?

— LEASE ON LOVE

#doseoflove

Love does not leave, it grows and transforms into something different.

STOP WAITING FOR LOVE! CREATE IT, LIVE IT, BE IT!

LEASE ON LOVE

DYING WILL COME NATURALLY, BUT THE COURAGE TO LIVE AND LOVE DOES NOT!

#doseoflove

Control often robs us of an unfolding experience.

#doseoflove

Hell is not to love anymore.

-George Bernanos

The solution to the problem lies in the problem.

—

LEASE ON LOVE

#doseoflove

"I don't know," is often really..."I don't want to say."

—Staci Bartley

Don't let anyone tell you differently...you matter!

#doseoflove

What robs us of the love we desire, are the fears we fondle and snuggle with at night.

-Staci Bartley

If love was absent, you would not feel disappointed; you would feel indifferent.

@LEASEONLOVE

What trips us up is what we cover up.

–Staci Bartley

#doseoflove

You only fail at creating love if you quit!

Following your heart and following your emotions are two different journeys. Which one are you on?

—

LEASE ON LOVE

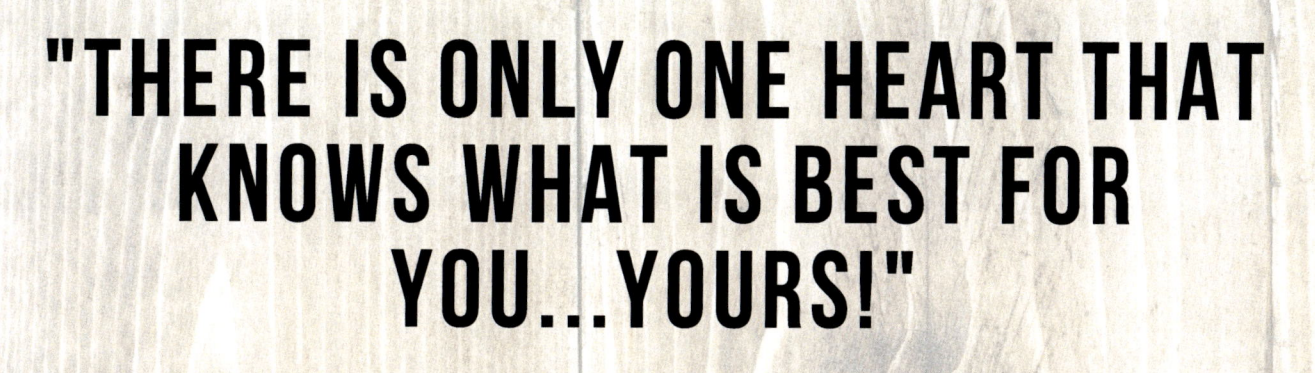

"THERE IS ONLY ONE HEART THAT KNOWS WHAT IS BEST FOR YOU...YOURS!"

#doseoflove

Acknowledgment and fun are the two gems necessary to get your relationship back on track.

NERVOUSNESS IS A SIGNAL THAT SAYS, "PREPARE FOR EXPANSION."

#doseoflove

When things are falling apart, please know they are actually falling into place.

If you enjoy having the opportunity to make a choice, you must give others the chance to do the same!

LEASE ON LOVE

#doseoflove

Admit there is a leak before there is a flood.

Beauty happens the moment you decide to *be yourself.*

LEASE ON LOVE

#doseoflove

Have WILD imaginings, and then ask for ALL of them!

Dating doesn't have to suck! Set your intentions for what you want to get out of it.

—

LEASE ON LOVE

#doseoflove

Relationships take skills, not perfection or LUCK!

MANY OF US DREAM OF TRAVELING TO UNKNOWN LANDS,
BUT THE THRILL AND EXCITEMENT OF

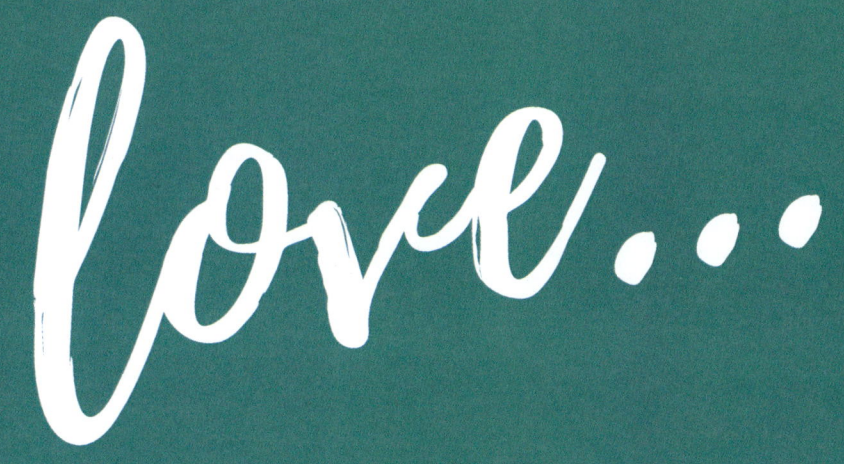

love...

NOW THAT WILL TAKE YOU PLACES!

LEASE ON LOVE

#doseoflove

The feeling of "should," is judgment in ACTION!

-Staci Bartley

"FORGET the RULES, because there are NO rules with LOVE!"

—

STACI BARTLEY

#doseoflove

Stop being paralyzed by fear and start having difficult conversations.

If you want to know where your heart is, look to where your mind goes when it wanders.

LEASE ON LOVE

#doseoflove

Love never asks you to be something that you're not. Your insecurities are the ones who do that!

Choose to FEEL again, not only the grass under your feet, and the wind on your face, but the emotions of your soul.
STACI BARTLEY

LEASE ON LOVE

#doseoflove

Never let anyone dull your sparkle!

#doseoflove

Awareness + Action = HOPE

FUEL YOUR PASSION BY GIVING IT ATTENTION.

#doseoflove

There is nothing wrong with allowing yourself to get into hot water...as long as you emerge cleaner for it!

Be STUBBORN with your deal breakers, and FLEXIBLE with your desires.

—

LEASE ON LOVE

#doseoflove

You can endure anything with a heart full of love...but love needs time for talking and touching to keep it alive and flourishing.

Is your intuition wrong? Or is it just opening a door you didn't expect?

LEASE ON LOVE

#doseoflove

We need others, not to make our decisions, but for a fresh perspective and a bit of inspiration!

THE ONLY RELATIONSHIP THAT IS GUARANTEED TO LAST FOREVER IS THE ONE YOU HAVE WITH YOURSELF! FOR BETTER OR WORSE!

#doseoflove

A quick fix will rob you of a journey into yourself that will ultimately produce some of your greatest treasures.

Look BACK, Don't Go BACK.

DON'T FORGET TO JOIN US FOR A CHALLENGE EXPERIENCE!

Bring these words to life by joining us for an upcoming challenge experience.

You can receive daily inspiration and a new Dose of Love every Wednesday, by following us on Instagram @leaseonlove

AND

Join us for one or more of our challenge experiences taking place several times a year.

Our challenge experiences offer you fun and simple ways to create more love and connection in your life!

Please join us for an upcoming challenge by visiting: thedailydoseoflove.com

CONNECT WITH US!

Let's be friends!

You can connect with us here:

Facebook: facebook.com/leaseonlove/

Twitter: @_leaseonlove

Instagram: @leaseonlove

Blog: leaseonlove.com/blog/

Made in the USA
Columbia, SC
28 March 2022